C Programming Language

A Step by Step Guide to Learn C
Programming in 7 days

Darrel L. Graham

C PROGRAMMING LANGUAGE
Copyright © 2016 by Darrel L. Graham

The contents of this book may not be reproduced, duplicated or transmitted without direct written permission from the author.

Under no circumstances will any legal responsibility or blame be held against the publisher for any reparation, damages, or monetary loss due to the information herein, either directly or indirectly.

Legal Notice:

This book is copyright protected. This is only for personal use. You cannot amend, distribute, sell, use, quote or paraphrase any part or the content within this book without the consent of the author.

Disclaimer Notice:

Please note the information contained within this document is for educational and entertainment purposes only. Every attempt has been made to provide accurate, up to date and reliable complete information. No warranties of any kind are expressed or implied. Readers acknowledge that the author is not engaging in the rendering of legal, financial, medical or professional advice. The content of this book has been derived from various sources. Please consult a licensed professional before attempting any techniques outlined in this book.

By reading this document, the reader agrees that under no circumstances are is the author responsible for any losses, direct or indirect, which are incurred as a result of the use of information contained within this document, including, but not limited to, — errors, omissions, or inaccuracies.

Table of Contents

Introduction 4
Chapter 1: What Is The C Language? 5
Chapter 2: Setting Up Your Local Environment 14
Chapter 3: The C Structure and Data Type 20
Chapter 4: C Constants and Literals 33
Chapter 5: C Storage Classes 40
Chapter 6: Making Decisions In C 52
Chapter 7: The Role Of Loops In C Programming 59
Chapter 8: Functions in C Programming 63
Chapter 9: Structures and Union in C 69
Chapter 10: Bit Fields and Typedef Within C 77
Chapter 12: C Header Files and Type Casting 90
Chapter 13: Benefits Of Using The C Language 98
Conclusion 102
Resources and Attributions 103

INTRODUCTION

C Programming Language introduces you to the most commonly used programming language, one that has been the basis for many other versions over the years. It is a great book, not just for beginning programmers, but also for computer users who would want to have an idea what is happening behind the scenes as they work with various computer programs.

In this book, you are going to learn what the C programming language entails, how to write conditions, expressions, statements and even commands, for the language to perform its functions efficiently. You will learn too how to organize relevant expressions so that after compilation and execution, the computer returns useful results and not error messages. Additionally, this book details the data types that you need for the C language and how to present it as well.

Simply put, this is a book for programmers, learners taking other computer courses, and other computer users who would like to be versed with the workings of the most popular computer language, C.

CHAPTER 1:
WHAT IS THE C LANGUAGE?

C Programming is one of the most useful and easy to use computer programming languages. The person who came up with this C Programming went by the name of Dennis M. Ritchie, and he worked at Bell Telephone Laboratories. At the time, precisely in 1972, C Programming was meant to help in improving the now widely used UNIX operating system, whose development had begun in 1969. And did it? Yes, it did. Its kernel code now began to use fewer lines than it did before when it used the assembly programming language, which is commonly abbreviated as *asm*.

That does not mean that the C language is restricted to only a few lines. It can actually take as few as three lines or as many as millions of them. At the same time, it is written in a single text file or a number of them, the text files bearing the extension, 'c', as in, *hello.c*.

As for its introduction to the market, the C programming language was not available to the public until 1978 when Ritchie joined hands with Brian Kernighan to produce the first set for commercial use. That is where the now common term, *K & R standard*, was derived from – Kernighan and Ritchie. It is important to point out that the C programming language was officially formalized by the *American National Standard Institute*, abbreviated as ANSI, in 1988.

Other Early Projects Improved By C

Oracle

UNIX was not the only project to be made more efficient by the C Language. The Oracle database also benefitted when, in 1983, its initial code that had been written in *asm* was re-written in the C language. The development of the Oracle database had begun in 1977.

Windows 1.0

Windows 1.0, which was released in 1985, is said to be partially written in C and partially in assembly or *asm*. The source code is, however, not available to the public.

The Linus kernel

The Linux kernel, which was released in 1992 as a composite part of the GNU operating system, and whose development began in 1991, also uses the C Language. Although some of GNU's components use Lisp programming languages, it still has others that use the C programming language. Incidentally, any idea what GNU represents? Well, apparently, IT is not all serious stuff without fun – GNU is … Wait for it… *'GNU's Not Unix'* - some artistic thinking there.

Anyway, for practical purposes, C language is more procedural than anything else and can be used for different operating systems. It is actually the most used so far worldwide, though it faces great competition from Java, another popular programming language.

Who uses the C Programming Language today?
The C Programming language is mostly used by software developers or programmers and particularly those using the operating system, UNIX, C compiler, and virtually every application program of UNIX. Suffice it to say, the C programming language is today the most used professional language in the world of computers.

Modern systems based on C Programming
The C Programming language, as has been stated before is still widely in use. It cannot pass as a programming language of old just because it helped to upgrade ancient programs. As this book will show, despite software experts having developed other programming languages, C is still in great demand.

Here are some modern systems still based on C:

1. Microsoft Windows
The Microsoft Windows operating systems dominate the computer market, taking around 90% market share. And their kernel is written in the C programming language for most part, fewer parts being written in *asm*.

2. Linux
Linux is another system written in the C programming language. This is significant because, in addition to Linux being used in personal computers, it is also the system used by the world's topmost supercomputers; actually the top 500 of them. Just to bring it home better, here are the 10 leading supercomputers in the world, part of the list of computers using the C language:

(i) Tianhe-2

Tianhe-2 is the name of the world's most powerful supercomputer. It is owned by the *National Supercomputer Center*, which is in Guangzho, China. This great computer was built in China by the *National University of Defense Technology*, abbreviated as NUDT.

(ii) Titan

This one joined the top league after being upgraded in 2012. Its location is *Oak Ridge National Laboratory* in the US, and its user is the *United States Department of Energy*.

(iii) Sequoia

This is another US supercomputer, and it is located in Lawrence Livermore National Laboratory in the state of California. It has been used largely in matters of climate, energy, as well as astronomy.

(iv) K Computer

The K Computer is a product of Fujitsu, who built it at the Advanced Institute for Computational Science (AICS). This institute is within RIKEN, Japan's biggest research institution, situated in the city of Kobe.

(v) Mira

This is another of US's supercomputers. It is located within the *Argonne National Laboratory*, which is at the outskirts of Chicago, and is largely used the *US Department of Energy*.

(vi) Piz Daint

This one is to be found in Switzerland, precisely in its southern city of Lugano. It is located at the Swiss National Supercomputing Center. Europe does not have a more powerful supercomputer than this one.

(vii) Shaheen II

This supercomputer is located at the King Abdullah University of Science and Technology in Saudi Arabia, and is the newest amongst the top 10, having gone live in 2015.

(viii) Stampede

This one is located within the Texas Advanced Computing Center in the US.

(ix) Juqueen

This supercomputer, which is found in Germany, is Europe's second to make the list of Top 10. It is located within *Forschungszentrum Juelich*.

(x) Vulcan

This is a US supercomputer located within the Lawrence Livermore National Laboratory.

3. Mac

The Mac is entirely run on C, including its drivers and programs, and that applies on all its models, just as happens in Windows and the Linux.

4. Mobile Phones

When it comes to the Windows phone, the android, and also the iOS, their kennels are in the C language. In short, their kernels are written just like those ones in the computers described above, only they are mobile adaptations.

5. Databases

Most databases used in financial systems; telecommunications; entertainment; health and education systems; the general web and elsewhere; are mostly written in C; or even C++. These include the most popularly used, like the Oracle, MySQL, MS SQL Server, and even PostgreSQSL.

Main Advantages of Using the C Programming Language

1) It is a structured language
2) It is relatively easy for someone to learn from scratch
3) It is efficient in the writing of programs
4) It does well in different computer platforms
5) It also does fine with low-level activity.

Everyday Use of C

It may be helpful, for the sake of beginners, to provide a breakdown of where the C programming language is most commonly used. The C language is actually easy to find, not just in Operating Systems, but also in Language Compilers; Assemblers; Text Editors; Print Spoolers; Network Drivers; Language Interpreters; Utilities; Network Drivers; and as already mentioned, in modern programs and databases.

Suffice it to say, the C programming language is very popular with writers of modern software applications, some of which are used in 3D movies and embedded systems like those used in TVs, remote controls, and so on.

Taking the example of a common utility item, the motor vehicle, here are some of its features that have been programmed in the C language:
1) The automatic transmission
2) The systems that detect the vehicle tire pressure
3) The sensors that monitor the levels of oxygen, temperature and oil
4) The various memory categories, including that of mirror settings
5) The dashboard display
6) The anti lock brakes
7) The vehicle stability control, which is automatic
8) The cruise as well as the airbag controls
9) The child proof locking system
10) The climate control

The motor vehicle example is just one among other utility items that have systems written in C. Even many vending machines from where you buy soda have C language systems. Many cash registers at shopping stores are also run in programs written in the C language.

What these devices that make life relatively easy have in common are embedded systems that run like small computers that have program running microprocessors written in C. That is why the systems detect it when someone presses a key and they react in ways pre-set. They also display relevant information accordingly. Many manufacturers of utility items prefer to have programs written in the C language because it has features that allow for flexibility; enhance efficiency; and which are compatible with many types of hardware.

Why Bother Learning The C Programming Language?
Is C the only programming language accessible to users today? Of course not! There are other programming languages that programmers and other computer users can learn and utilize, some low than C, and still some higher and more modern than C. So why C…?

There are other reasons for wanting to learn the C programming language, besides the ones already mentioned in this book. First of all, the C programming language existed long before many other computer languages were ever thought of. As such, it has built a rich source code base. In short, you can learn a lot and there is a rich pool of resources to tap from in this regard. C also has lots of functions that you can use to meet your program needs.

At the same time, for the same reason that the C programming language has been in use for a long time, you are unlikely to find challenges in its use that you cannot get solutions to fast. Users of C have, over the years posted questions over the internet and received solutions from other users as well as experts, and you can learn a lot about C from those discussions. In addition, there are many tutorials provided free on the web, and those too make it relatively easy for someone with interest to learn the C language.

Another plus for C is that it is the computer language that UNIX uses, and UNIX is among the leading computer software. Other great operating systems use the C programming language as well. For that reason, C has become more like the lingua franca of the programming world. It is also worthwhile noting that the way C expresses ideas makes it easy for users to appreciate them and also implement them with little or no support.

Something else that would encourage you to learn the C programming language is that it has been the basis for other computer languages, and many other languages have picked something worthwhile from C. You will, for example, find some principles and some commands being in use in C and also in use in other computer languages. What this means that you can share tips with other programmers who use other languages and communicate easily with them too.

CHAPTER 2:
SETTING UP YOUR LOCAL ENVIRONMENT

It often helps to have a strategy when trying to learn something new. In the case of learning the C programming language, it is imperative that you proceed from the basics to the more complex aspects. That is why it is a good thing we began the book by laying out the beginnings of C and how it has helped build other programming languages.

Preparing To Learn The C Programming Language
It is a good idea to begin by downloading and then installing the compiler. The reason you need to do this early is so as to have a program that can interpret your C code, and converting it into computer friendly signals.

Is there a universal compiler available?
The answer is in the negative, as there are some programs that are suitable for Windows and not great with other operating systems, or great for Linux and not very good with other operating systems.

Here are some helpful suggestions:
- Install Microsoft Visual Studio Express, or even MinGW, if your computer is running on Windows.
- Install XCode in case your computer is running on Mac
- Install gcc if your computer has Linux as the operating system

As has already been noted, you can write a C program in lines as few as three or as many as you wish. The text files need to have the extension, ".c". You can, for example, write *hi.c*, when your source statement contains, *hi*. To write your C program, you use a text editor like *vi*, *vim*, *Emacs* and such others. Essentially, you use a text editor to enter your statements from the source to the program, using your chosen language, say, the C programming language.

IBM is known for using *XEDIT* as their text editor, and operators who use UNIX systems are known for using *Emacs* as well as *vi* as their preferred text editors. For fresh starters, *vi* stands for visual editor. In accomplishing laying out commands, it uses keystroke combinations in place of menus, making it faster than most other text editors. You may also like the *Pico* text editor if you are entirely new in using UNIX systems.

Setting the Environment
In this chapter, you are going to learn how to set up your C programming environment, if that is the way you want to go. Otherwise, if you simply want to test how successful you are in writing in the C language, you can log onto;
http://www.compileonline.com.

In setting the environment required for the C programming language, you need to ascertain that the computer you are using has two specific software tools, namely, the text editor and the C compiler.

(1) Role of the text editor tool
This is the tool to use when doing the actual typing of your program. Besides the text editors already mentioned, like the *vi* and the *Emacs*, there are others like the *Windows Notepad*, the *OS Edit command*, *Epsilon*, and even *Brief*.

When you use a text editor, what you create goes by the term, *source file*, and what it contains are the *source codes* for your program. As noted earlier, C programs have the extension ".c".

The text editor is so basic to programming that you cannot begin doing any programming without a text editor ready for use. However, with your chosen text editor ready, you write your computer program; next you save it in form of a file; and after compiling it, you execute it.

(2) Role of the Compiler
What, exactly, is a compiler? Well, you can term it a computer program, though sometimes its make-up is a combination of more than one computer program. What is its role in the C language? The role of the compiler is to make the source file you have created usable by your computer. In short, as it is initially, the source code that you have written in your source file is the human readable source that is now contained in your program. Yet you would like that source code put into binary form, which is what your target computer language is made of. Once you are done, you will have translated your source code into object code, the term used after the process.

So, a compiler effectively compiles your source code into your chosen machine language, making it possible for your computer's CPU (Central Processing Unit) to execute your instructions, and finally producing executable programs. You will often have a ready compiler on the net, which you can use free of charge. Many programmers prefer using GNU C/C++ compiler, although, depending on the operating system one has, some go for HP and sometimes Solaris. The reason you see C and C++ put together is that what works for the C language also works for C++.

Installing your GNU C/C++ compiler:
It is not surprising to find the compiler already installed on your system, particularly when your computer is using either Linux or UNIX, so it is good to check before proceeding to install afresh.

Checking If Your Computer Has The Compiler
How do you check? Simple – after opening a terminal, try and locate, say, your Linux C compiler. And the way to do this is by using the *which*-command: *$ which gcc*. If your machine actually has the C compiler, you will, very likely, see the output, */usr/bin/gcc*. That /usr/bin is, obviously, a directory.

Now, to see the compiler version that you have, you need to type, *$ gcc –v* as your command, within the command line available. Just in case your computer already has the compiler you are looking for, the message you will receive will look like this:

Using specs already built in
Target: i386-redhat-linux

Configured with: ../configure --prefix=/usr ....
Thread model: posix
gcc version 4.1.2 20080704 (Red Hat 4.1.2-46)

Installing a Linux/UNIX Compiler

Suppose your computer does not have the compiler installed? Well, you will have to do the installation yourself. Luckily, it is an easy process. All you need to do is log onto *http://gcc.gnu.org/install/*, and follow the simple guidance provided on the site.

Installing The Mac OS X Compiler

However, in case your computer is using the Mac OS X, and not Linux or UNIX, you can log onto the apple website, developer.apple.com/technologies/tools/, and then download the relevant code, which happens to be *Xcode*. The site gives instructions that are easy to follow, so installation of your *Xcode* development environment should be relatively easy. After you have the environment ready, you will be in a position to make use of the GNU compiler in relation to the C programming language.

Installing the Windows compiler

What you need to do in case your computer is using Windows, is to log onto *www.mingw.org*, which is actually the homepage for *MinGW*, and by clicking on the link provided you will be able to download the *MinGW*, which is the compiler you need for your computer. During the process, you should be able to ascertain that you are downloading a version of *MinGW* that is current – the latest. Just to be sure you are downloading the correct program, see that it reads something like: *MinGW-<version>.exe*.

Note too that there is a minimum set of programs you need to download for Windows if you want to have your compiler working as required. They include *gcc-core; gcc-g++; binutils*, as well as *MinGW* runtime. You could install others as well, but those mentioned make the bare minimum. Remember to include to the PATH variable the sub-directory, *bin*, as you install your MinGW, reason being that it will help you specify tools in the command line just by looking at their names, which are relatively simple. After successful completion of your installation, you should be able to run the tools you downloaded right from the command line – tools like the *gcc; ranlib*, and the rest.

CHAPTER 3:
THE C STRUCTURE AND DATA TYPE

It is important that you know how the structure of C looks like at the bare minimum, before you can proceed to learn what its main building blocks are. Once you know these basics, they will become your reference points as you learn more about the C language.

Here are the basic components of the C program:
1. The pre-processor commands
2. The functions
3. The variables
4. The Statements as well as Expressions
5. The comments

Example

Let us use our example: "Hello, learners!" What code could we use to print those words?

(i) First of all, you would have your first program line as: #include <stdio.h>, being your pre-processor command.

(ii) Your next would contain: *int main()*, being the program's main function; and that is where the program begins to execute commands.

(iii) The line that follows is: /*...*/. The compiler usually ignores it because it is where you are meant to add your comments if you so wish. You call such lines simply *comments*. Just for illustration's sake, you could enter the comments: /* *beginning to learn C */*.

(iv) The next line that follows is: printf(…); and that is the line that enables your message, "Hello, learners!" to appear on your screen. So, essentially, after your entry, you will have: printf("Hello learners!\n")

(v) Finally, you have the next line returning the value 0 and terminating the main function, ().

Compiling and Executing the C language program

At this juncture, you need to learn how to go about saving your source code, and also running it. Remember we mentioned entering your source code so that your computer's CPU can process it accordingly.

The easy steps to follow:
- Get your text editor open, and then type in the source code that you have
- Next, save your file in the name of *hello.c*
- The next action is opening a command prompt and moving to the specific directory where you have just saved your file.
- Once there, type, *gcc hello.c*
- Tap enter after typing that and you will have compiled your code
- In case your process has been good and you have no errors within your code, you will be prompted to proceed to the line that follows. After this, you will see an executable file generated – *a.out*
- You now need to type *a.out* to have your program executed.
- Everything having gone well, you should be able to view your output – *Hello learners!* – displayed on your screen.

- So, basically, what you should be seeing on your screen is something like this:

> $ gcc hello.c
>
> $ ./a.out
>
> Hello, learners!

Basic C Syntax

For any process to work well, and for you to be able to issue the right commands, you should be able to identify every item for what it is. That will avoid confusion and minimize errors. For that reason, in C programming, you need identifiers.

What, Exactly, Is An Identifier?

In C language programming, an identifier helps you to locate a variable; a function; and any other item that you, as the user, may have defined. You will see an identifier beginning with an alphabet – anywhere from A up to Z; and sometimes an underscore: '_', which is then followed by a zero and sometimes letters or more underscores. Sometimes digits, anywhere from 0 to 9, may follow.

Note:
- When using the C language programming, you cannot use punctuation like @, %, £, and such, within your identifiers.
- The C language is also case sensitive. In other words, the lower case cannot respond to the upper case situation. For example, learners and Learners are recognized as two entirely different identifiers.

To make it more clear, below are some identifiers that are acceptable when using C:

abc; hername30; a40c9; retVal; _temp; a

In C language programming, there are some words that you cannot use at all whether as constants, as variables, or as identifier names. They are said to be reserved keywords.

Reserved keywords in C include *auto, else, long, switch, break, enum, register, typedef, case, char, extern, float, return, short, union, unsigned, const, continue, for, goto, signed, sizeof, volatile, default, do, int, if, struct, static, packed, while* and *double*.

Use of White Space in C
If there is a line that is entirely blank, the compiler automatically ignores it. Such a line is termed *white space*. However, *white spaces* are not restricted to blank spaces alone. They also include newline characters (e.g. \n) as well as tabs and comments.

Does a white space accomplish anything in the C programming language? Yes, it does. It shows the end of one statement element and marks the beginning of another. In short, ordinarily a statement is made up of different parts, each carrying some meaning; and those parts combine within the statement to convey some information. For that information to be understood in the C language, and with precision, you need to input your text in a way that the compiler will identify each bit for what it is.

Example:

When you have an expression like *int main*, the only way the compiler is going to recognize *int* and *main* correctly is by having some whitespace character separating them. In such a case, space is the most commonly used. However, there are situations where you are at liberty to either use whitespace or leave it out altogether.

Example:

In the statement, dessert=cream + candy; //get the entire dessert, you can include some space between dessert and the equals sign or leave it out altogether. Likewise, you can put space between the equals sign and cream or leave it out. In such instances, you would be expected to use your discretion in a manner to enhance readability. Otherwise, whether you use the whitespace or not will not affect the way the compiler picks that part of the statement.

Types Of Data In C

Why is type important when it comes to a programming language? Well, there are different reasons, including the storage space some types occupy on your machine as opposed to others. In the C programming language, there are data types that represent variables whereas others are used to declare functions. The type of data does not just determine storage space but also the manner in which its bit pattern is understood during processing.

Here are the main data types in C:

(1) The Basic

The basic data type in C is also referred to as the primary data type.

It includes the arithmetic type, which is further categorized as integer, abbreviated as *int*; floating, usually represented as *float*; and character, usually represented by *char* and sometimes *void*. When void is specified, it means that no value is being returned or reflected; and as for the integer, they represent variables.

Here is a simple table to demonstrate how the basic data type is categorized:

Basic/Primary Type of Data				
Character	*Integer*		*Float*	*Void*
	signed	*unsigned*		
Char	*Int*	*int*	*float*	
signed char	*short int*	*short int*	*double*	
unsigned char	*long int*	*long int*	*long double*	

Note that the integer data type stores whole numbers. In this regard, taking a 16-bit computer as an example, the signed int takes up two bytes; the unsigned int takes up two bytes; the signed short int takes up one byte; while the signed and unsigned long int take up space of four bytes each.

When it comes to the float type of data, plain float takes up space of four bytes; the double takes up eight bytes; while the long double takes up ten bytes.

And as for the character type of data, which basically stores the value of characters, signed char takes up space of just a byte, and the same case applies to the unsigned char.

The void type of data ordinarily represents functions that produce no value whatsoever. Sometimes these are functions that do not accept any parameters.

As has been noted, functions in the C language whose return type is void are those returning no value. Here is how they look like:

void exit (int status)

Again, there are those functions in C that accept no parameter. However, a function not accepting parameters can, nevertheless, accept void as in the example below:

int rand(void)

(2) Derived
Under the derived type of data are functions; various data structures; and also pointers.

What could pointers be?
Well, a pointer happens to be a variable that has an address of another variable. It gives direction as to where that other variable is, helping to recall the contents of that other variable. You need to realize that pointers have nothing to do with object type. Take the following function, for example:

*void *malloc(size_t size)*

This function, which obviously has a pointer to no other value but void, is one that can always be casted to any type of data you have. Remember to always declare your pointer before beginning to use it for storage of whatever variable address you want. Below is a demonstration of the general form you use for pointer declaration:

type *var-name;

Type, in this case, stands for the base type of your pointer, which needs to be a valid data type used in the C language. var-name is the pointer variable's name. You need to know that although the asterisk used is the same one you ordinarily use for multiplication, within the C language you use it to mark the designation of the variable as pointer.

Real examples of pointer declarations:

int	*ip;	/*pointer to an integer*/
double	*dp;	/*pointer to a double*/
float	*fp;	/*pointer to a float*/
char	*ch;	/*pointer to a character*/

Note that whether you are entering pointer values that are integers or character; float or even double; what cuts across them all is the requirement that the value be one long number that is hexadecimal, and which is a representation of the memory address. Otherwise the pointers only differ in the specific constant or variable data type that each of them points to.

When you are doing your variable declaration, if you have no particular address to assign to the pointer variable, assign it a null value so it becomes a NULL pointer. You can refer to it as a pointer with zero value. In many operating systems (OS), programs will not access address 0/zero; the OS simply reserves it.

Pertinent Details Pertaining To C

Pointers are of fundamental importance in the C programming language, the reason every programmer needs to be aware of its basic concepts. Luckily, they are concepts that are easy to learn and to remember.

Below are the pointer concepts and their explanations:

1. The pointer arithmetic	The C language has a choice of 4 arithmetic operators to choose from when creating a pointer; namely, ++; --; + and -
2. Pointer arrays	An array does not hold a singular pointer but a number of them.
3. Pointer to pointer	The C language enables you to create a pointer on another pointer
4. Passing a pointer to a particular function	You do this by declaring your chosen function parameter in pointer type. Any function accepting a pointer also accepts an array of pointers.
5. Returning pointer from function	This involves allowing a function to actually return a pointer to a variable that is local, static, and one with memory that is dynamically allocated.

Clarification of Pointer to Pointer

This is a case of having pointers in a form of chain. Ordinarily what you have is a pointer with a variable address. However, with a case of pointer to pointer, the pointer you create first has an address of your second pointer. That second pointer, in turn, has the location where the actual value you want is. You are required to always declare when you have a pointer to pointer variable. And how do you do that? Well, you add one more asterisk next to the usual one that you place before the pointer name. Then you end up with something like this:

int **var;

Still, what, exactly, are Variables?
Variables come up often in conversation, and they appear in many functions, not least in the C language. When it comes to the C programming language, a variable is simply a representative of storage area. It is the place where programs in C perform their manipulations. Practically, you can use variables to store various data value. Variables are different from constants because as you execute your program in the C language, you can alter your variables, something you cannot do with constants. During programming, you may give your variables names that have ordinary meaning, like *height* or *weight*; *age*; *average*; and such.

It is important to note that variables are of specific types and the type of each determines its memory size as well as its layout. It also determines the value range that can be accommodated within the memory. The variable type also determines the particular operations that you can apply to the variable in question.

How do variables look like? Well, they come in form of digits; also

letters, as well as the underscore. And you need to declare them before you begin using your program for two major reasons:
a) So that the compiler can recognize the name of the variable
b) So that it can be aptly categorized – given its appropriate data type

Also when defining a variable in the C language, you need to follow some stringent rules.

Variable related rules:
- Provide a variable name that does not exceed eight characters
- The name you provide should not have a digit at the beginning
- Do not include blanks or any space within your chosen variable name
- Use digits or alphabets; and even special symbols such as underscore (_) as you wish in creating a variable name.
- You cannot use keywords to represent variable names

In fact, whenever you are declaring names of variables or for functions, or you are declaring your constants, be keen not to include a C keyword.

Incidentally, what are keywords within the C programming language?
The C keywords are grouped as *auto*, *double*, *int* and *struct*. Normally, the compiler will do the categorizations of the keywords, the keywords essentially making part of the C syntax. C keywords

are actually pre-defined and so you just need to know which ones they are.

Take the example: *int cash*

Cash happens to be the variable, and its type is integer. The keyword indicating cash then is *int*.

What You Need To Know About Keywords In C:
1. In C, keywords are also referred to as *reserved words*.
2. The keywords used in C are 32 in number.
3. You need to learn the specific C keywords so that you do not use them as variables in functions.
4. When using a C keyword, you are required to assume the meaning the compiler has provided or defined for that keyword.

Here are the 32 keywords used in C programming:

auto
The C keywords under auto are specifically *break; case; char; const; continue; default;* as well as *do*. These plus *auto* make a total of eight.

double
Under double are the keywords *else; enum; extern; float; for; goto* as well as *if*. These plus *double* make a total of eight.

int
The C keywords under int are *long; register; return; short; signed; sizeof;* as well as *static*. These ones plus *int* make a total of eight.

struct

The C keywords under struct are specifically *switch; typedef; union; unsigned; void; volatile;* as well as *while*. These keywords plus *struct* add up to eight.

CHAPTER 4:
C CONSTANTS AND LITERALS

In the C programming language, the term literal can also be used in place of constant. Now, what, exactly, is a constant in the context of C programming? Well, it is the term used for a fixed value in the data being entered in the program, which the program cannot alter in the course of execution. Constants come in all data types – floating, character, integer and even string. You can also find constants of enumeration.

When it comes to actual C programming, you use constants in the same way you use regular variables; only that with constants you would not be able to modify their values after you have defined them.

What would happen if you tried to alter the value of a constant? Simple: The program will return an error message. After clarifying the nature of constants, let us go through some basic rules that will help in using them.

Rules to observe in constructing constants in C:

(1) Integer Constants
  a. Every integer constant needs to have a digit
  b. No integer constant should have a decimal
  c. It is alright for an integer constant to be either positive or even negative
  d. You must not add a comma or even a blank anywhere within your integer constant

e. Whenever there is no sign preceding an integer constant, the assumption is that the constant is positive
  f. For the sake of processing in your computer program, when you are selecting your integer constants, the range you have to work with is from -32768 to 32767.
(2) C language real constants
  Incidentally, these are the same ones we referred to earlier as *floating point constants.*
  a. Each of them also needs at least a single digit
  b. It is also necessary that it contains a decimal
  c. Just like with integer constants, it is acceptable as positive or negative
  d. Here too, in case you do not put a sign before the constant, it is interpreted as being positive
  e. And as for commas and blanks, here too they are not acceptable.
(3) Character constants
  a. This one comes in singular: one alphabet, one digit, or even one special symbol. In short, its length is always one character.
  b. A character constant is enclosed within a single quote
(4) String Constants
  a. A string constant needs to be enclosed in a double quote.
(5) Backlash Characters
  a. In the C programming language, you use a backlash character when it carries a special meaning
  b. You also use the backlash here to denote the character's special function

Let us analyze the various literals that exist in C.

The Integer Literals

These ones are usually decimals, octals, and sometimes hexadecimals. They bear a prefix that actually defines the base. For example, Ox (OX) marking a hexadecimal, 0 indicating octal, and of course nil marking a decimal.

You can also have a suffix on an integer literal, for example, *U* combined with *L* to denote *unsigned* and *long*, in that respective order. You also need to appreciate that when it comes to the suffix, both the upper and lower cases are acceptable.

Here below are some great examples of literal integers:

078	/*Illegal: 8 is not an octal digit*/
215u	/*Legal*//*
032UU	/* Illegal: cannot repeat a suffix*/
212	/*Legal*/
OxFeeL	Legal*/

Additional examples of varied integer literals:

85	/* decimal */
30	/* int */
30u	/* unsigned int */
0213	/* octal */
Ox4b	/* hexadecimal */
30l	/* long */
30ul	/* unsigned long */

35

The Floating Point Literals

Floating point literals have combinations of parts – some integers, others decimal, some fractions, and still some exponents. When it comes to representation, these literals are shown in decimal; otherwise exponential.

In times when your literals are coming in decimals, you need to remember the decimal point; and sometimes both the decimal point and the exponent. Then when the literals are coming in exponential form, you need to factor in the integer; fraction part; and sometimes you add the part that is fraction to that integer. Note that your signed exponent needs to be preceded by an *e* or *E*.

Here is some demonstration of floating point literals:

510E	/* Illegal: incomplete exponent */
3.14159	/* Legal*/
314159E-5L	/* Legal*/
.e55	/* Illegal: missing integer or fraction */
210f	/* Illegal: no decimal or exponent */

The Character Constants

Character literals come in single quotes, for example, 'x'. The character literal is then stored as a char type; just being one simple variable. You need to note that although it is fine to have simple character literals, sometimes you are called upon to create an escape sequence.

Example of such an escape sequence:

'\t'), or just a universal character like '\u02C0'.

Something else worth noting is that you can vary the meaning of a character constant just by preceding it with a backlash. Good examples are the newline, which is represented by *\n*; and the tab, which is represented by *\t*. In short, you can have character literals being plain characters, as in *x*; escape sequence, as in *\t*; and even as universal character, as in *\u02CO*.

Further Demonstrations of Escape Sequence Codes:

Escape Sequence Codes	Meaning
\\	\character
\'	'character
\"	"character
\?	?character
\a	Alert (or bell)
\b	Backspace
\f	Form feed
\n	Newline
\r	Carriage return
\t	Horizontal tab
\v	Vertical tab
\xhh ...	Hexadecimal number of one or more digits

Example of 'Hello, learners' in Escape Sequence

#include <stdio.h>
int main()
{printf("Hello\tlearners\n\n"); return 0}

The escape sequence code after execution

After the sequence code above has been compiled and also executed, the result you get is as follows:

Hello   learners

The String Literal

As for the string literals or string constants, you need to know that they are enclosed within quotes, as in (""). That string has characters that are plain, escape sequence or universal. Something else worth noting is that the characters in string literals never come in singular; always as two or more.

Ordinarily, you begin your string literal with a backlash (\); and then you follow it up with characters that will determine the ultimate interpretation of your escape sequence. Just for example, if you want your computer to bring out *newline*, what you type as your escape sequence is \n.

As for the universal characters, they are those that represent Unicode code points within the string literal. These are the ones you write like \uxxxx or \Uxxxxxxxx. *X* in this context represents one hex digit. What we are essentially saying is that you have the escape sequence, \uxxxx playing the role of marking or representing *xxxx* as the code point.

Although string literals are sometimes long, you have an opportunity to break them by the use of white spaces. Here below is an example of three ways you can break one literal string, so that you end up with the same string in three identical forms:

| "hello, learners" | "hello, \ learners" | "hello, " "l" "earners" |

Manner of Defining Constants

When it comes to defining constants for use in the C language, this is done in two main ways:

(i) By a pre-processor: *#define*

(ii) By a keyword: *const*

Pre-processing is the first thing that happens compilation is going on in the C program. It is a feature strictly unique to C language programming compilers. It is also important to note that every directive being undertaken by the pre-processor begins with #. By *directive* here we mean *command*.

The benefits that come with the C pre-processor include:
- Easy process of developing programs
- It is relatively easy to read
- It is similarly easy to modify
- Its C code is easy to transport to varying machine architectures.

CHAPTER 5:
C STORAGE CLASSES

What does a storage class got to do with the C language? Storage classes in C actually play a big role in the name declaration syntax. A storage class indicates the scope the variables cover and also the duration they are to remain stored – what you can call their lifetime. It also controls its linkage. In the C programming language, storage classes are four.

Here are C's storage classes:

1. Auto

This is C's default storage class for every local variable. Its storage duration is automatic and it operates within functions.

2. Register

The term register is used here because the storage class specifier prompts the compiler to put the object in question within the register in the processor. As for storage, the duration here is also automatic. The uniqueness with the register storage class is that it helps identify any local variable that needs to be stored within the register as opposed to being held within RAM (Random Access Memory). This automatically means that the size of your variable cannot exceed that of the register. Ordinarily that size which is meant to fit the register is only a single word; without adding something like & as there is no memory location for it.

3. Static

This is the same one sometimes referred to as *thread* storage. Its storage is static and has internal linkage. What this static storage class does is give indication to the compiler that the local variable needs to be spared as long as the program lasts. This is as opposed to it being destroying it when it gets out of scope. Owing to this manner of functioning, the variables retain their exact values in between function calls.

4. Extern

This one is similar to static storage, with the difference being in its linkage, which happens to be external. It is the one that enables a global variable to be visible in every program file. However, you cannot initialize the variable if it is 'extern' but it will direct you to the relevant storage location. This happens usually in situations where you have created multiple files. What happens is that you define a global function or a global variable, and when checking out another file, you will see 'extern' being used to give direction or reference to the variable already defined; or even function.

What is linkage in C? It is simply a name denoting object, value, reference, template, function, namespace, or even type.

Operators in C

In the C language, an operator is that symbol – and they are a number of them – that directs the compiler to do specific functions of a mathematical or logical nature. Some of C's operators are in-built.

Categories Of Operators In C

(1) Arithmetic

These are specific and so it is easy to learn and remember them. We shall list them here below and demonstrate how you apply each of them. For our demonstration, we shall assume that variable A has the value of 20, while variable B has the value of 40.

Operator	Operator's Function	Practical Example
+	To put together two operands	A + B = 60
-	Reduces the 1st operand by the value of the 2nd one.	A – B = -20
*	Multiplies the 1st and 2nd operands	A * B = 800
/	Divides the numerator by the denominator	B / A = 2
%	One operator divided by the other and the remainder is the result	B % A = 0
++	Role of increasing integer by 1.	A++ = 21
--	Role of reducing integer by 1.	A-- = 19

(2) Relational Operators

These ones help you to determine the block to follow, once you compare the values between two variables already in storage.

Here are further examples using the same two variables, A = 20 and B = 40.

Operator	Operator's Function	Practical Example
==	Verifies if two operands have equal value; if not, condition is returned as not true.	(A ==B) is not true
!=	Verifies if two operands have equal value; if not, condition is returned as true.	(A !=B) is true
>	Evaluates if left operand has greater value than right operand; if so, condition is returned as true, otherwise untrue	(A > B) is not true
<	Evaluates if left operand has less value than the right one; if so, condition is returned as true	(A < B) is true
>=	Evaluates if left operand has value that is greater or equal to the right operand; if so, condition is returned as true, otherwise, not true	(A >= B) is not true
<=	Evaluates if left operand has value that is less or equal to that of the right operand; if so, condition is returned as true, otherwise, false	(A <= B) is true

(3) Logical Operators

There are basically three logical operators that the C programming language supports. Assuming that A is one of your variables and its value is 1; and B is the other one of your variables and its value is 0; this is how the program works:

Operator	Working Explanation	Practical Example
&&	This one is named the *Logical AND Operator*. If the 1st as well as the 2nd operands happen to be non-zero, you will have the condition returned as true	(A && B) is false
||	This one is named the *Logical OR Operator*. It means that if either of your two operands happens to be non-zero, you will have the condition returned as true.	(A || B) is true

(4) Bitwise Operators

These operators work by manipulating data right at the bit level. They also shift bits from the right position to the left. Note that bitwise operators do not work with C's float variables or the double float variables.

Let us first observe the various roles of the different bitwise operators:

Operator	What Operator Stands For
&	Bitwise AND
|	Bitwise OR
^	Bitwise exclusive OR
<<	Left shift
>>	Right shift

Here below is a table showing the workings of three bitwise operators: &, | and ^:

a	b	a & b	a | b	a ^ b
0	0	0	0	0
0	1	0	1	1
1	0	0	1	1
1	1	1	1	0

What is essentially happening in our table above is that the left operand is specifying the value that needs to be shifted; while the right operand is specifying the actual number of positions those bits within the value need to be shifted. And that is how it generally works with bitwise operators.

When it comes to the bitwise exclusive OR, otherwise abbreviated as *XOR*, what happens is that the exclusive OR operation considers two inputs and returns 1 (one) if either of those inputs is 1 (one). In short, it cannot return 1 if both of the inputs are 1; or if both of them are 0. If it so happens that you have both inputs as 1, or you have both of them as 0, then, the operation will return 0.

(5) Assignment Operators

The C language supports a number of assignment operators. Below are the assignment operators that C supports and how they work:

Operator	What The Operator Does	Example
=	Allocates values from operands on the right to those on the left	m = n
+=	Adds the value of the right operand to that of the left operand; then assigns the resultant value to the left operand	m += n means that m = m + n
-=	Here it subtracts the value of the right operand from that of the left operand; then assigns the resultant value to the left operand	m -= n means that m = m - n
*=	The left operand gets multiplied by the right operand; and the product is then assigned to the left operand	m *= n means that m = m * n
/=	The value of the left operand is divided by that of the right one; then the result is assigned to the left operand	m /= n means that m = m/n
%=	Here the operator takes the left and right operands and uses them in modulus calculation; then gets the result assigned to the left operand.	m %= n means that m = m % n

(6) Conditional Operator

This operator also goes by the term *ternary* operator. Conditional operators play the role of evaluating conditional expressions. See illustration below:

46

Operator	What The Operator Does	Example
?:	An expression is provided; and the operator represents the condition that if expression 1 is true, value 1 is assumed; otherwise value 2 is taken.	If condition true ? then value y, otherwise, value z

(7) Special Operators

Each special operator is different from the others, each performing its unique function. Here below are the main special operators in the C programming language:

Operator	Operator's Role	Practical Example
&	Locates the variable's address	& y returns y's actual address
*	Acts as actual pointer to the variable	*y is the actual pointer to variable y
sizeof	Provides the variable size	sizeof (y) returns variable y's size

Precedence Of Operators In The C Programming Language

In the use of C programming language, whenever terms are grouped in an expression, each of those terms is evaluated. As a result, some are given precedence over others depending on the operators therein. There are, obviously then, those operators that are accorded higher precedence over others. Just to cite a simple example, the operator of multiplication takes higher precedence over that of addition.

Let us try another example:

Given y = 5+3*4, what would you give as the answer?

If you have no idea about precedence, you might be tempted to go the linear way, adding 5 to 3 and then multiplying their sum by 4; in which case you would have 32. However, this is not correct in C programming where the multiplication operator is higher in precedence than the addition operator. So the correct way is to multiply 3 by 4, whereby you will get their product as 12; then add 5 to 12 and you get 17. That is the same way you are expected to treat different operators within the same expression – according to the precedence each has in C.

Below is a table showing the precedence of various operators in descending order:

1. Operators taking the highest precedence: number one overall:
   a. A suffix and postfix, being increment as well as decrement ; from left to right, that is, ++--
   b. A function call, which is, ()
   c. An operator of array subscripting, which is, []
   d. An operator of structure, as well as union member access, which is.
   e. An operator of structure as well as union member via pointer, and that is, ->
   f. The compound literal or C99, which is, (type){list}

All the above operators have left to right associativity; or you can call it fixity. It is indication of how you are expected to understand precedence in each case even when no parenthesis is used.

2. Operators taking the second position in precedence
   a. A prefix increment as well as decrement, both denoted by ++--
   b. Unary plus as well as minus, both denoted by +-
   c. The logical NOT as well as the bitwise NOT, both denoted by !~
   d. The type cast as denoted by (type)
   e. Indirection, or otherwise, dereference, represented by *
   f. Address-of, represented by operator, &
   g. The size as denoted by *sizeof*
   h. Requiring alignment, or otherwise, C11; and that is represented by *alignof*

   The associativity of this category of operators is right to left.

3. These are the operators coming third in precedence

   They include operators of multiplication, of division, and any remainder; and they are considered from left to the right. They are denoted by */% and have associativity of left to right.

4. Here are operators taking fourth position in precedence. They comprise those of addition and also subtraction, as denoted by +-. Here too, associativity is from left to right.

5. The operators taking precedence in this fifth position have associativity of left to right. They include the bitwise left

shift as well as the right shift. The operators themselves are <<>>

6. The operators taking this sixth position in precedence include relational operators, which are:
   a. < as well as <=
   b. > as well as >=

So, essentially, the operators in play are <<= and >>= with associativity of left to right.

7. Seventh in order of precedence are other relational operators.

They are specifically ==!= and their associativity is also from left to right.

8. Eighth in order of precedence is the bitwise AND, simply denoted by &.

This, too, has associativity of left to right.

9. Ninth in precedence is the exclusive bitwise operator OR.

This is the one denoted by the operator ^; and it has left to right associativity as well.

10. Tenth in order of precedence is bitwise OR, which you can term the inclusive OR. It has left to right associativity also, and it is the one denoted by the operator, |

11. Eleventh in line is the Logical AND. This one also has left to right associativity. It is denoted by &&.

12. The logical OR follows in order of precedence in twelfth position. Its associativity is also left to right. This operator is denoted by ||
13. This operator that is thirteenth in precedence is the ternary conditional. It is denoted by [note 1] and its associativity is right to left.
14. The operators that take fourteenth position happen to be simple assignment
    a. This is an assignment of sum as well as difference and it is denoted by +=-=
    b. Another one is assignment involving product and quotient; as well as remainder. It is denoted by *=/=%=
    c. In, this category too is bitwise assignment, which happens to comprise the left as well the right shift. These are denoted by << = >>
    d. There is also another bitwise assignment, and that involves there operators, which are AND, also XOR, and lastly OR; denoted as &=^=|=
15. The last one in line, ranking 15th, is the comma, and its associativity is from left to right. It is denoted by ,

CHAPTER 6:
MAKING DECISIONS IN C

What does decision making entail within the context of C language programming? Well, you need to know the best order to execute certain expressions or statements provided; or those you have personally designed. There is a way you can lay out your statements and your program fails to return any usable results; possibly returning errors. Some sets of statements actually require repeating before they can meet the conditions needed. As a programmer, the reason you go to these lengths is to be able to make pertinent decisions relating to your programming. The true or false results that your program returns are very important because they come about through a thorough process of evaluation. Essentially what C does is help you weigh different conditions against one another, in a bid to solve one or more problems that you are faced with.

As a programmer using C, you are expected to be able to specify one condition, or even more, which the program will evaluate and test. These are handled together with a given statement or a select set of statements, and they are then executed if the condition or conditions you specified prove to be true. Otherwise, if the condition or conditions do not prove to be true, meaning they are proven as false, the alternative statements may be executed.

The C language handles decision making in a simple but organized manner. Here are statements that C supports for the sake of decision-making:

(1) The *if*-statement
(2) The *switch* statement
(3) The *conditional operator* statement
(4) The *goto* statement

How The *if*-Statement Works:
This one comes in four different forms as shown below:

a. The simple one
This one simply mentions one condition or supposition and states that something specific is going to happen if that supposition holds true. However, if that supposition does not hold true, the suggested thing does not occur; rather the situation becomes different. In programming, and in this case C, you need to put that situation in form of a statement, so that your program can evaluate the condition and execute commands appropriately.

Here is how you express it:
- *If (your chosen expression) {this inside statement;} this outside statement*

b. If…else
In this statement, you have two specified possibilities, so that if your expression does hold true, your first statement works; or else, which essentially means your expression failing to hold true, your second statement works. You could also have a situation where, should the condition be true, the program executes a set of statements; and if the condition is not true, the program executes a different set of statements.

Here is how you express it in readiness for execution:
- If (your chosen expression) {1st statement;} else {2nd statement 2}
- If (your chosen condition) {1st statement; 2nd statement;} else {3rd statement; 4th statement}

c. If…else; nested

This one is very near like *if…else,* only that it has a third alternative statement. Here is a situation where you may find it necessary to insert an if-statement or *if…else* statement right within another.

Here is how you express a nested if:
- *If (your 1st condition) {1st statement ;) else _ if (your 2nd condition) {2nd statement ;} else 3rd statement.*

d. Else…if ladder

In this form of statement, you have your chosen expression tested starting from the upper part of the ladder and progressing downwards, and in the process trying to verify the condition present. Only if the condition is found as expected is the related statement executed.

Points worth Noting:
- In C, values that are non-zero or non-null are the only ones that can hold true. So, for a value that is zero or even null, the program automatically returns results as false.
- You can have one single statement within the if-statement that is not enclosed in curly braces – {}

See this example:
> Int a = 6
> If (a > 5)
> Printf ("success")

As you can see, no curly braces have been used in the above example, and none were needed. However, if the situation were different such that there was an additional statement within the *if*-condition, you would need to enclose those statements within curly braces.

- The operators, == need to be used carefully to avoid confusion between it and the = operator. The only time you can use == appropriately within an expression that has an *if*-condition is if you are making a comparison. Otherwise the = operator in such an environment executes an assignment; not at all a comparison.
- Anything you enter as condition in an if-statement will hold true if it is not a nil/zero (0) value

Example:
if (25)

Printf ("hi");

In this particular example, you can be sure to see *hi* printed.

What you have been using all along as the syntax of the *if*-condition is the Boolean expression. And what, exactly, is the Boolean expression? Simple: It is the expression you use in programming to produce a Boolean value after evaluation. By value here we simply mean the *true* or *false* results we have mentioned elsewhere in the book. In actual fact, these two alternatives – *true* and *false* – are values of the Boolean data type. They are the outcome of logic when working with Boolean algebra.

And what would we say Boolean algebra is? Well, it is simply a branch of algebra that deals with the variables of truth; denoting *true* and *false* in terms of *1* and *0* respectively, as the case may be. The first person to initiate this algebraic system that deals with logic mathematically went by the name of George Boole; the reason the terminologies of Boolean value, Boolean expression and so on are in use today. As you can deduce, being able to return values through logic is very important because it means any decision you are going to make on the basis of those values has a solid basis. It means you are certain what conditions are bound to work and which ones are bound to fail. Hence it is fair to say that C helps in making verified data based decisions.

How the *switch*-Statement Works:
Just like the if-statement, the switch statement also influences a program's flow in case the condition being tested proves to be true. One thing you need to note about the *switch* statement is that it sometimes has varied conditions. The way it goes is that if the statement has a variable that meets the first condition contained in the *switch* statement, whatever command there is goes through and is executed. In fact, you can enter a default within a *switch* statement but it is not mandatory. In case you have included a default, and all the variables within the *switch* statement fail to meet the condition given, the default you have in place takes place.

In practice, switch statements come in handy in solving problems of a multiple-option nature; especially when dealing with a program like a menu, where you have particular values associated with specific options.

How the *conditional operator*-Statement Works:
You can denote the conditional operator like this:?: *operator*

This is a statement that you can use in place of the *if...else* statement. Here is an example of the form this statement takes:

Exp1 ? Exp2 : Exp3;

Each of these – Exp1, Exp2 and Exp3 – is an expression on its own. It is important that you do not forget to put the colon in its right position as illustrated above.
How to determine the value of any given expression within the statement:

(i) Evaluation of Exp1 takes place first.
- What happens if it is found to be true? Evaluation of Exp2 immediately takes place. At the end of the day, it is the value of Exp2 that is taken as the entire expression's value.

(ii) Evaluation of Exp1 takes place first.
- What happens if it is found to be false? Exp2 is ignored, and instead evaluation of Exp3 is immediately takes place. The resultant value of the entire expression is that of Exp3.

How The *goto*-Statement Works

This one actually alters the conventional sequence of C programming. It is known for instigating a jump on unconditional basis, to a location within the function where there is a labeled statement. What happens then is that you can easily lose trace of the program flow; and that is not a good thing as it makes it difficult for you to modify the program even if you so wanted. Suffice it to say, there are experts who discourage programmers from using the *goto* statement.

CHAPTER 7:
THE ROLE OF LOOPS IN C PROGRAMMING

What, exactly, is a loop? Within the context of C programming, a loop is that programming function that enables iteration of a statement, or of a condition, on the basis of specific boundaries. Incidentally, the way loops work is more or less similar across different programming languages.

Notably, when you are working with a given statement, or with a set of instructions, execution continues until such a time as a specified boundary condition – the anticipated loop body – is met. Thereafter, repetitions of that initial cycle of operation can continue, involving the whole loop body, until execution of the entire code block is accomplished as required. Still, on the overall, you get statements being executed in a sequential order. In short, if you have more than one statement in the same function, the program executes the first statement first; the second one follows; and so on. It is worth noting that you can have different execution paths even when they are complex. The main reason loops are important in programming is that it is their statements that facilitate execution other statements severally.

Different Loops And How They Work:

1. The *while loop*
The *while loop* operates while a certain condition happens to be true, repeating a statement or set of statements. It actually performs

the evaluation of the test expression. It then ensures the condition is tested before it can execute the loop body. However, if the test expression proves to be false, what follows is the termination of the *while loop*.

This is how *while loop* syntax looks like:

while (condition) {statement;}

Note that the statement needs not be one; there could be more.

2. The *for loop*

In this loop, execution of the initialization statement occurs just once. What follows immediately after is the testing of the expression. If ever it is found false, returning zero (0), the loop gets terminated. However, in case the result returned is non-zero, meaning the test has proven the expression to be true, the codes within *for loop* are automatically executed. Also the expression gets an update. After several repetitions of this process, the expression being tested finally turns false. You need to note that you use *for loop* mostly when you have a known number of iterations.

This is how *for loop* syntax looks like:

For (init; condition; increment) {statement;}

Here, too, the statement can be more than one.

3. Do…while loop

This loop is works almost similarly to how the while loop works but for one difference. Its body gets executed even before it can check the test expression. It is only after that initial execution that the evaluation of the test expression takes place. In the event that the test expression is proven to be true, the do…while loop's body gets executed once again. The repetition process then continues till such a time as the test expression returns a zero (0) value; meaning it turns false.

This is how *do…while loop* syntax looks like:

do { statement; } while (condition);

You need to take note of the position of the statement – not at the end as in other loops, but right at the beginning; preceding the condition. Reason…? As pointed out earlier, the statement within the *do…while loop* must, of necessity, execute at least one time before it is time to test the condition. Hence the condition in this loop comes last.

4. Nested loops

You are dealing with nested loops when you find yourself with loops within the other loops already mentioned – the while; the do…while; or even the for loop.

    a) This is how a *nested for loop* syntax looks like:
       for (init; condition; increment) { for (init; condition; increment) { statement; } statement }

    b) This is how a *nested while loop* syntax looks like:
       while (condition) { while (condition) {statement;} statement; }

c) This is how a *nested do...while loop* syntax looks like:

Do { statement; do { statement; } while (condition);

5. The infinite loop

Would you envisage a situation where a given condition never has a chance of turning out false? Such are the situations that call for the use of the *for loop*. Of course, of the three for expressions, none will be required. So, what you end up with is an endless loop simply because your conditional expression will, certainly, be empty. That is how you end up with an endless – or *infinite* – loop. And just in case you feel like terminating your infinite loop, simply press the keys, *Ctrl* + *C* simultaneously.

Chapter 8:
Functions in C Programming

How would you define a function? Well, for the purposes of the C programming language, a function may be termed as that set of statements that perform tasks as one and not as independent statements. You will find a function in every C program, even if it is just a single one. Essentially what you always have is a main function. Other functions then come in as additions defined by trivial programs that may be present. If you so wish, you can look at a function as a code module that readily takes in information – the kind of information that comes in symbolic names conventionally referred to as parameters – then processes some computations, and often returns some fresh information. Of course, the information a function returns depends on the captured parameter information.

Anything unique about the main function? Yes, there is. Although in handling you treat the main function just like any other function, it is unique in that it is the only function that the operating system needs working whenever you, as the computer user, begin running your program. In short, every time you begin running your machine, the first code to be executed is the main function.

Here is how the main function structurally looks like:

Int	//if successful, expect to return a zero (0)
Main ()	//this is the place for the name, which, in this regard, is main
{}	//this is the place for numerous codes; being the function body

In C, a code is divided into diverse functions and you can do the division as you wish. However, for the purpose of logic, you need to distribute your code amongst the functions at hand in a way that leaves every function performing a defined task. You actually need to take every C function as a major building block within your program. Simply put, every C program that you have working is written through the use of functions. This is done so that the program can be used repetitively and with consistent efficiency, and also to make it better understood.

As you continue working on C programming, there are some terms that you will come across and you need to know their meaning in the relevant context. One of those terms is *function declaration*. What is it?

Function declaration
Do you recall what a function is? A function declaration, on its part, is responsible for instructing the compiler on the function name, the return type, as well as the function parameters. And the function body is actually derived from the function definition.

Here is the form that a function definition generally takes in C:
Return_type function_name(parameter list) {function body}

Here below are the components of a function definition, including the header and the body, which are the main parts:
1. Return type
It is anticipated that a function will return a value; and it actually

may. Now, that value is of a certain data type. That data type is what we refer to as *return_type*. However, as you may have already noted, there are some functions that go well within the program, yet they do not return a value. This is the scenario where we declare that the *return_type* is void – *void* being one of C's keywords.

2. Function name
This is the exact function's name.

3. Parameters
First of all you need to realize that you do not have to work with parameters when it comes to functions in C programming. However, when you have them, it is important to know what they constitute. You can actually take a parameter the way you do a placeholder. What happens is that the minute you initiate a function, you give the parameter some value. It is this value that you can cite as being the actual parameter; or alternatively, the argument.

From the parameter, you get a parameter list; and this one is in reference to the type; the order; as well as the actual number of parameters the function has. If you then add your parameter list to the function name, what you get is the function signature.

4. Function body
When it comes to the function body, what you will find in it is an assembly of statements defining what the actual function is all about.

Why Use C Functions?

Let us summarize why it is important to use C functions:
   a) To save yourself the repetitive task of re-writing the program's code or logic
   b) You can call on the C functions any time you need a similar functionality
   c) You always have access to the program anywhere and anytime, thanks to the functions that keep the program stable and working consistently even when your machine is off.
   d) Functions make it possible and easy for you to track a huge C program. This is because you are not faced with plain massive data but data that is broken down in logical functions.

How C Function Works

The C function has three distinct aspects, namely:
   (i) The prototype, which you can also term function declaration.

   What this one does is keep the compiler informed on the issues of function name; the function parameters; as well as the return value of the data type. The syntax for the function declaration is:

   return_type function_name (argument list);

   (ii) The function call
   This is the caller of the real function. Its syntax is:

   function_name (arguments list);

(iii) The function definition

This is where you find the entire set of statements requiring execution. The syntax for the function definition is:

return_type function_name (arguments list) { body of function; }

You need to remember that it is important to declare a function and to clearly define it before you can proceed to call in a C program.

Calling a C function

When it comes to calling a C function within a program, the best way to go about it is:

(i) Calling it by value

(ii) Calling it by reference

Calling a C Function By Value

(i) When it comes to calling a C function by value, you have the variable's value passed right to the C function in its parameter state.

(ii) As you make your call, you need to note that you cannot modify the real parameter value through the formal parameter.

(iii) It is important to appreciate during your calling of the C function that the actual parameter and the formal parameter have varying memory.

You also need to take note of the difference between the actual parameter and the formal parameter. Here lies the primary difference:

The actual parameter is effectively the one used in the course of a function call.

- The formal parameter happens to be the argument that you use within the function definition.

Chapter 9:
Structures and Union in C

The general meaning of C structures as represented by the C keyword, *struct*, is a data type declaration of a complex nature, which defines a variable list whose items are grouped under a single name within a memory block. It makes it convenient to reach individual variables through just one pointer.

As such, when we speak of structures in the C programming language context, we are referring to a data type that is user defined, and which facilitates combination of data items that are varied in nature. Structures effectively stand for records just the same way you safeguard literature in libraries. This enables you to track down details about the book title, the author and such other pertinent details.

Here is the syntax of struct:

Struct *structure_name { //statements};*

In case you want a C structure that reflects the dictionary name, its prices as well as its number of pages, you could have it as follows:

Struct **Dictionary** *{ char name [15]; int price; int pages; };*

How To Define C Structure

It is necessary to utilize the *struct* statement in defining the structure of the C language, a statement that is good at defining fresh data type that happens to have in excess of one member. Important to note too is the fact that it is optional to use a structure tag. As you do your definition, you need to appreciate that every member definition is an ordinary variable definition, as exemplified by *int i; float f,* and such other valid definitions that are variable based. Before you insert the semi-colon, you are at liberty to specify additional structure variables. Being at liberty, of course, means that you do not have to.

When you want to declare structure variables, remember it is all right and doable to declare the variables after you have completed defining the structure itself. Act

Declaring Structure Variables
It is possible to declare variables of a **structure**, after the structure is defined. **Structure** variable declaration is similar to the declaration of variables of any other data types. Structure variables can be declared in following two ways.

Getting Access To Structure Members
How do you access structure members? You accomplish this by using what is known in C as *member access operator*, which is coded as period (.). That code exists right between the name of the structure variable and the very structure member you are trying to have access to. The keyword to use in trying to define any variable of the structure kind is *struct*.

Just to alert you, a structure can pass for a function argument in C, just as you do with other variables or even pointers. Here is an example:

#include <stdio.h>

Relating Pointers With Structures

It is also possible to define a pointer to a structure just as you are able to define a pointer to a variable of any kind. Here is a fitting example:

*struct dictionaries * struct _pointer;*

Hereafter you can always store the particular address associated with a structure variable within the pointer variable just defined above. What you need to do in order to locate the actual address associated with a structure variable is to place the operator, &, right before the name of the structure.

Here below is a fitting example:

Struct_pointer = &dictionaries1;

To succeed in accessing the members of any structure by use of a pointer associated with the structure, you need to make use of operator, ->.

Here below is a suitable illustration:

struct_pointer->title;

Bit Fields

What are they? Bit fields is generally a term applied, within the computer programming arena, to encompass storage of multiple neighboring bits that bear logic; also in situations where sets of bits as well as single bits are easily addressed. The bit field often represents integral kinds of already known bit=width, one that is fixed in nature.

Another thing you need to know about bit fields is that they facilitate data packing within a structure. This comes in handy particularly in times when data storage or the memory in general, is at a real premium. You will find more details pertaining to bit fields later in the book.

Union in C

Do you recall that a computer has storage space in which to store data? Now that is very central in explaining what union in the C programming language is because union happens to be some special data type, which facilitates taking into the computer memory varied data types. In C, union is almost similar to structure; actually being more like a derived mode of structure. In fact, the main difference you will see is in the definition, and only on the part of the keyword. Whereas you use *struct* when defining structure in C, with union in C the keyword you use is *union*.

Still, you need to note that even when the union comes with a number of members, it is only one of them that can bear value at any one time. Suffice it to say, it is the union, this special data, which enables the memory to work with efficiency even as it handles different tasks.

You can define a union this way:

union car { char name [20] ; int price ; } ;

In order to appreciate better what a union is, you need to take the union statement into account, where you will notice the new data type being laid out with its numerous members, all helping in running your program.

Below is the union statement format:

Union [union tag] { member definition; member definition; ... member definition; } [a single or several union variables];

Something else you need to note is that it is optional for you to use a union tag. You also need to know that every one of your member definitions is basically an ordinary variable definition, such as, *int i; float f;* or any of those other variable definitions that are valid.

How would you define data of a union type that bears three members, *i, f,* as well as *str*?

To accomplish this, you need first of all to have it clear in your mind that the minute you finalize the definition of the union, and even before you can insert your ending semi-colon, there is room to specify a union variable, or even multiple of them. Note you have room to do that but you are not obliged to do it – it remains optional.

Here is how you define the data with three members:

union data { int i; float f; char str[20]; } data;

What becomes clear is that your data type variable is capable of storing an integer, a floating point number, and sometimes even a whole string of characters. So you end up having that one variable that is, certainly, in a single memory location, being utilized as storage for multiple data types. Gladly, it is possible for you to utilize a built in data type of your choice, or a user defined data type within a union, all depending on the prevailing requirement.

Another important thing to know is that you need not worry about accommodation of a large union member because the memory a union occupies happens to be sufficient to accommodate the largest of your union members.

If you consider the example provided immediately above, the data type is ready to occupy memory space of 20 bytes; reason being that 20 bytes happens to be the maximum space that a character string can occupy. If you would like to know the size of the entire memory that the above union has occupied, here it is:

#include <stdio.h> #include <string.h> union data { int I; float f; char str[20] }; int main( ) { union data data; printf("data occupied memory size : %d\n, sizeof(data)); return 0; }

When whatever is up here above, meaning the code, has been duly compiled and actually executed, the result you receive is very simple. Here it is:

data occupied memory size : 20

How To Access Union Members

In order to access a union member, what you use is what is referred to as member access operator. And while this might sound technical, the member access operator is simple to understand because it is coded, (.) – a period. This period appears right between the name of the union variable and the select union member; the one you are trying to access. In defining union type variables, the keyword you need to use is *union*.

Illustration on using unions within your program:

#include <stdio.h> #include <string.h> union data { int i; float f; char str[20]; }; int main( ) { union data data; data.i = 10; data.f = 220.5; strcpy(data.str, "C programming"); printf(data.i: %d\n", data.i); printf(data.f : %f\n", data.f); printf("data.str : %s\n", data.str); return 0; }

However, the way this illustration is, the members of the union, *i* and *f,* could have their values corrupted because the final value has taken up the entire memory. You could get the following results after code compilation and execution:

data.i : 1917853763
data.f : 4122360580327794860452759994368.000000
data.str : C Programming

Solution…? Use one member at a time.

Illustrating how best to use unions within your program:

```
#include <stdio.h> #include <string.h> union data { int i; float f;
char str[20]; }; int main( ) { union data data; data.i = 10; data.f =
220.5; strcpy( data.str, "C programming"); printf( "data.str :
%s\n", data.str); return 0; }
```

In this latter illustration, you have opted to use one member only, giving it priority, and as a result, you will have every union member now printed properly. After the code has been compiled and also executed, here is the result you are bound to receive:

data.i : 10
data.f : 220.500000
data.str : C Programming

CHAPTER 10:
BIT FIELDS AND TYPEDEF WITHIN C

Bits are essential in managing data storage in your machine. That is the reason structure, as well as union members, has their sizes specified in bits. What you want is to be able to utilize the storage at your disposal as efficiently as possible because it is in no way infinite. It is limited in scope and capacity and you need to be able to operate successfully within the limited range.

Take a situation where the C program you have has some variables that are either true or false, and they are all grouped in a single structure named status. In short, suppose you had the structure looking like the illustration below:

> struct { unsigned int widthValidated; unsigned int heightValidated; } status;

Bit Field Storage
Ordinarily what you do is establish the variables within a structure, thereafter you define each variable's width, and that informs the C compiler the precise number of bytes you need to utilize. Here is an example of how you can write the structure from the illustration above:

> Struct { unsigned int widthValidated : 1; unsigned int heightValidated : 1; } status;

To be clear, you need in total 4 bytes for the status variable's memory space. However, practically, you are only going to use up 2 bits because they are sufficient to store the values you have in the illustration above. In C, classes as well as structures can have some members occupying less storage space than a major type. Such are the members referred to as bit fields.

Bit field can be used to reduce memory consumption with the knowledge that it is only some bits which will be used for the variable. Bit fields allow efficient packaging of data in the machine memory.

The obvious fact is that an integer takes two bytes (16-bits) in memory. Sometimes we need to store value that takes less than 2-bytes. In such cases, there is wastage of memory. For example, if we use a variable temp to store value either 0 or just 1. In our current scenario, only a single bit of memory is going to be used rather then 16-bits. By using bit field, we can save lot of memory.

What you use for creating bit fields in C include *unsigned int; signed int,* and sometimes *Bool* when it comes to C99. You begin by setting up your bit field using structure declaration, which basically labels every field and also ascertains what its width is. After this, the compiler packs all the bit fields in adjacent location and which are of uniform type, and ends up reducing the number of words. This subsequently drastically reduces the storage space required for the bit fields. In short, you can credit the bit fields with allowing data packing into a structure.

For instance:
- Numerous objects can be packed to form a machine word. For example, it is possible to compact 1-bit flags
- It is also possible to read file formats of a non-standard nature; or those with external file formats. A good example is reading 9-bit integers.

The way the C programming language enables this is through structure definition, where you can put: bit length somewhere following the variable.

A suitable illustration:

struct packed_struct { unsigned int f1:1; unsigned int f2:1 unsigned int f3:1; unsigned int f4:1; unsigned int type:4; unsigned int my_int:9; } pack;

There are six members in total in the above illustration. They include four 1-bit flags, which are f1, f2 as well as f3; a single 4-bit type; and also one 9-bit *my_int*. It is C that then conveniently packs those bit fields in a compact manner.

It is important to know also that C allocates bit fields within integers starting from the one that is least significant to the one that is most significant. Let us observe the code below:

struct mybitfields unsigned a : 4; unsigned b : 5; unsigned c : 7; } test; int main(void) { test.a = 2; test.b = 31; test.c = 0;

This is how C would arrange the bits:

00000001 11110010
ccccccbbbbbaaaa

Typedef Within C

Are you familiar with the tact of using an alias? While that may be common to people, it is not practically confined to human folk. The C language has a way of creating aliases for data types; and *typedef* is the keyword that helps in this process. Essentially what happens is that you give an entirely new name to your chosen data type. Sometimes the type name represented is a complex one.

Here below is an example:

You are required in this instance to provide a definition for the term, byte, for 1-byte numbers. The definition is:

typedef unsigned char BYTE;

The important part that follows now is that you can now use *BYTE*, which is, in this position, an identifier, taking it to be the abbreviation for the data type shown as *unsigned char*.

What you would have after processing is complete is:

BYTE b1, b2;

The uppercase in BYTE stands out. Why do we use the uppercase as opposed to the lowercase? Simple: It has always been the custom. However, this is not all. It is helpful to use the uppercase so that you are always reminded that this type name is actually symbolic – symbolic abbreviation. Still, nothing prevents you from writing your symbolic abbreviation in lowercase. In short, if you so wish, you could write your abbreviation as:

Typedef unsigned char byte

Typedef is also used to provide a name for data types that happen to be user-defined. You may, for instance, use a structure based *typedef* in defining an entirely new data type. Thereafter, you use the fresh data type in defining structure variables.

Comparing *typedef* to *#define*

The big question is: what is *#define* first of all? Only after we know what it is can we make a good comparison. *#define* is actually a C-directive. Next thing you should know is that it is also used in defining aliases for different data types. Can we call that a similarity with *typedef*? Sure, we can.

So, where does the difference between *typedef* and *#define* lie?

Well, you will find more than one difference when you compare *typedef* to *#define*. Here are the differences:
- Remember *typedef* provides symbolic names for data types? Although #define does this as well, it goes further to provide aliases for data values also. Incidentally, this is as simple as defining *1* as simply *ONE*.

- You will find the other difference right within the processing. In C, it is the compiler that determines what your *typedef* is all about; performing its interpretation. However, when it comes to your #define statements, it is the pre-processor that does the processing.

How would you use $define within your program?
Here is a good example:

Include <stdio.h> #define TRUE 1 #define FALSE 0 int main( ) { printf("Value of TRUE : %d\n". TRUE); printf("Value of FALSE : %d\n". FALSE); return 0; }

What is the result after compilation as well as execution of the code? Here it is:

Value of TRUE : 1
Value of FALSE : 0

Chapter 11:
Input Output (I/O) In C

Is this, by any chance, the conventional input and output that are found in various processes? Well, the input and output here may well be associated with a process, but they are not necessarily conventional in the real sense. In C, the two happen to be facilitated by some functions that are in-built within the program; the functions being *printf()* and also *scanf()*.

In order to appreciate what input means in C, after mentioning that it is the act of feeding data right into your program, you need to know that input sometimes comes as a file. Other times it emerges from some command line.

As far as output goes, you will be right to associate it with what you see on your computer screen; what comes out through your printer; or in general whatever data that comes into any of your files. When your data that has become your output does not appear on your screen, it is often saved within your computer in form of text or what is referred to as binary files.

One thing you need to know is that every time you have a program running that calls for the use of your keyboard or even your screen, certain three files automatically open. In fact, the C program has a way of treating every device as a computer file even when all you are interested in is displaying some data.

Incidentally, what do we name as file in C programming? In simple language, what you refer to as file is some disk space where you store grouped data. You could also look at a file as representing some byte sequence, irrespective of whether the file happens to be text or binary.

Why have files, anyway? Simple – to ensure your data is well preserved for use at a later time. If you terminate a computer program and you happen not to have a file, all the data you have been looking at, and probably working with, will be lost. However, once you create your file, your data remains intact all through, and all you need to do is give your computer a few simple commands and your file appears. In C, what you are bound to find in plenty are functions.

Here are two main categories of the high level Input/Output functions:
 (1) The text file
 (2) The binary file

The file functions in C are not complicated, so you will find them easy to learn. At all times, you need to get in touch with the *stdio* library for your functions to succeed. Of course, you have already seen it used in examples provided in earlier chapters of this book. The question at this juncture is: what exactly is in the *stdio* library? Well, what you may actually be interested in that is stored in the *stdio* library are the file functions involving input as well as output.

Here they are below:

(i) Fopen

This one performs the function of opening your text file.

You may find this prototype from *fopen* helpful:

FILE *fopen(const char * filename, const char * mode);

(ii) Fclose

This is the one that performs the function of closing your text file

(iii) Feof

This one performs the function of detecting your end-of-file marker in the file

(iv) Fscanf

The function performed by this one is reading the input from your file that happens to be formatted

(v) Fprintf

This one does the function of printing the file output that happens to be formatted

(vi) Fgets

This one undertakes the function of reading any string your file contains

(vii) Fputs

This one performs the function of printing any string required into your file

(viii) Fgetc

This is the one that performs the function of reading characters right from your file

(ix) Fputc

This is the one that does the function of printing characters right into your file

Dealing With File Opening In Case Of I/O Text File

This is the function denoted by *Fopen*. It is important that you know that besides opening your text file, this function utilizes a specific mode as it undertakes file opening. The three modes it often uses are:

- Read, denoted as *r*
- Write, denoted as *w*
- Append, denoted as *a*.

There are other modes besides the three already named, and they are as follows:

- The one used for reading as well as writing and is denoted as mode *r+*
- The one that does the opening of the text file for the purposes of reading as well as writing; proceeds to truncate it so that it reduces to a length of zero; or if no file exists proceeds to create one. This is the mode referred to as *w+*.
- This is the mode credited with opening your text file for reading as well as writing; and beyond that it engages in creating a file where none exists. On top of those functions borne by this same mode, it enables reading right from the

beginning while only facilitating appending when it comes to writing.

The way text file opening works is by the *fopen* statement opening file, "output.txt" within the write or w-mode. In cases where the function finds the file not existing, the file gets created.
However, you need to be cautious not to try creating a file when another one is in existence because if you do, the existing file gets destroyed and you are left with the new one.

As for the *fopen* command, it function is to return a pointer to your file, and that gets stored within the variable *ptr_file*. Just in case your file fails to open, you get the variable ptr_file returning NULL.*if(!ptr_file)*.

What then assesses if your file has opened is the *if-statement*, and that is executed only after *fopen* performs its function. How do you tell if or not your file has opened? Well, you will observe the program returning a one (1) in case *fopen* failed in its function of opening the file. Of course, this then becomes your indication that something is amiss and needs addressing.

Reading your text file in C
The function that reads your file content is the *fgets*; but that is only after you have successfully opened your file in *read* or *r-mode*. The *fscanf* function is also helpful in this situation, and that is on condition your file is well formatted.

When you want to prepare a file for reading, you open the file as "*input.txt*", and the function you apply for this purpose is *fopen*; the mode being read mode or r-mode. The process involves *fgets*, which is essentially a library function, reading every line comprising not more than 1,000 characters. Then in case *fgets* is successful in executing the function, which means it has read all the lines in the text file and reached the end of file, otherwise referred to as EOF, the value you should expect to see returned by *fgets* is NULL. What follows thereafter is the printing of every line on *stdout*, ordinarily on your screen, and it goes on till EOF comes. At this juncture, you would be fine instigating the closing command to bring the program to a successful end.

Dealing With File Closing: *Fclose(Ptr_File)*

The fclose statement closes the text file for you. If what you are doing is writing files, you should not expect this function to take place before you initiate it. So it is for you to instigate the *fclose* command at the time you deem appropriate. Something else, if in the course of typing your command you omit 'f' and type only 'close', the function will not operate. It is worth noting that the *close* command is entirely different from *fclose* in C programming.

You need to note that the *fclose* function, or *fclose()*, ordinarily returns a zero whenever it is successful. However, whenever it encounters an error while attempting to close the file, the result it returns is *EOF*. This EOF, though meaning End of File, happens to be also a constant, which is defined within *stdio.h*, a file in the header. There is also something else that this function does besides closing your file – it does flush any pending data, the one remaining in the buffer, and sends it into the file before closing the file.

Any danger if files fail to close in the right manner? Sure! If the affected files happen to be many, you run the risk of your program crashing. This is after failing to locate any remaining file handles, and probably, running out of memory space.

Dealing With *Printf*

When it comes to the printf statement, you should not expect to see the newline, \n, anywhere within the format string. The newline is rendered redundant by virtue of the *fgets* function adding the newline, \n, to each line end after reading it.

CHAPTER 12:
C HEADER FILES AND TYPE CASTING

What, exactly, is a header file? It is an important file in C programming, as it contains declarations as well as macro definitions, and those are shared amongst a good number of source files. What you do when you want to reach a header file in C is ensure you have included it in your pre-processing command or directive that you issue; and that is by typing '*#include*'. It is actually the same way you see the header file that comes with the C compiler having *stdio.h*.

The header file has an extension that is denoted as .h and it is the one that bears the declarations of the C function as well as the macro definitions. Headers in C come in two types, namely:
- Programmer written files
- Compiler attached files

When you include a header file, the impact of it is equivalent to having the header file content copied. Even then, you are discouraged from attempting to copy a header file's content because you would be risking creating many errors. The danger is particularly high in cases where your source files are many within the program.

Instead of attempting to work on the content in the header file, you need to adopt the accepted and widely used practice of keeping a select set of items in your header files. Those C items include:

- The constants
- The macros
- The global variables for the system
- The function prototypes

With these properly secured within the header file, you are at liberty to include that particular header file as and when you need to.

How The *include syntax* Works

In the working of the pre-processing directive, #include, you as the user, and your system header files, are brought together by the program. These are the two forms that the directive takes:

a) #include <file>

What this directive initiates is a search through specific system directories contained in a standard list. This search is meant to track down a file that bears the name, *file*. As a programmer, you are at an advantage as you can also pre-pend directories to the existing standard list. The way to do this is by using the –I option as you compile your own source code.

b) #include "file"

This happens to be the form you are meant to use for your header files whenever you are writing using own program. What it does is search for a specific file that goes by the name of file, and the place it searches is right within the directory with your current file. Here, too, you can pre-pend your directories to the list with the existing –I option as you compile your own source code.

How The *include operation* Works

This one, which you may also refer to as the *#include* directive, works by simply guiding the C pre-processor into scanning some specific file as your input, and then proceeding to work with the remaining part of the source file which is current.

As for the pre-processor output, it has varied categories of output as follows:
- The output generated at program initiation
- Output emanating from the file you have included
- Output emanating from text following execution of the *#include* directive

Let us take the example of a header file, say, *header.h*:

char *test (void);

And the main program using the header file is named *program.c*

This is generally what you would comprehensively have:

int x; #include "header.h" int main (void) { puts (test ()); }

In this case, the compiler will be seeing a token stream similar to the one it would see if it was *program.c* reading. See such a situation here below:

Int x; char*test (void); int main (void) { puts (test ()); }

Establishing One-Time Headers

You need to guard against having headers processed severally so that you end up with more than one header, which is basically an error. The way to do this is to include the header file only once; the only way there is to ensure the C compiler processes it once only. The question is how to go about ascertaining that you include your header file only that once. Gladly, there is a standard way of doing this, and it also happens to be simple. This standard method involves enclosing the entire file contents within a conditional.

See example here below:

#ifndef HEADER_FILE
#define HEADER_FILE
the entire header file file
#endif

This is how our example here, what is referred to as *construct*, works. It is generally known as wrapper *#ifndef*. When you find yourself including the header a second time, be sure the conditional will come out false. This is because the header file, (or HEADER_FILE), happens to be already defined. The processor, on the other hand, will efficiently ignore the file contents so that the C compiler does not get opportunity to see it a repeat time.

The Workings Of Computed Includes

It is practical to imagine that you may sometimes have several header files to choose from when you want to include one into your C program. However, there may be specifications to fulfill, like particular configuration parameters and so on. To be able to accomplish your task, here are some conditionals you may want to use:

#if SYSTEM_1 # include "system_1.h" #elifSYSTEM_2 # #include "system_2.h" #elifSYSTEM_3 ... #endif

Does this help you accomplish your mission? It sure does – but it brings along a problem. If you continue with the above conditionals, soon it is going to prove too tedious for comfort or even too clumsy for your concentration. So it is advisable to make use of the advantages of C, where you can use a macro to represent a header name; a function your pre-processor has enabled. When you do this, you speak of utilizing a *computed include*. In short, you do not write any header name anywhere, the way you would do as an #include argument. This is how to use a macro name:

#define SYSTEM_H "system_1.h" ... #include SYSTEM_H

Any idea what is going to happen? SYSTEM_H as you see it will undergo expansion. In the process, your pre-processor will be seeking out *system_1.h* just as would happen if your *#include* had been there all along, written as it is.

C Type Casting

What do you reckon type casting is within the context of the C programming language? It is one of the easiest things you will learn about C. For starters, you can define it as a means of converting a variable from what it is, to a different data type.

You may, for instance, wish to have a *long*-value integer into just a simple one. In such a case, you could typecast *long* onto *int*. Alternatively, you could do your value conversion from one integer to another by overtly making use of the cast operator.

You can also explain type casting as alteration of a particular expression associated with a particular type so that it now belongs to a different type. Type casting is a common thing in C language programming. It is generally advisable to alter lower data type turning it to a higher data type because that way you do not risk losing data. On the other hand, whenever you convert higher data type to a lower data type, you find your data having been truncated. Just to give you an idea, if you were to convert *float* to *int*, all data coming after the decimal disappears.

Another yet simpler explanation of what typecasting is indicates that it is one way of making a type of variable to behave as if it were another type. You can take an example of an *int* acting as if it were a *char*; and the behavior alluded to here is a one-time thing – only during the operation at hand. If you want an easy way to typecast, simply pick the variable type of your choice, and then put it within parenthesis before the variable whose behavior you want altered. For example, (char)a outright makes variable *a* to function as if it is a char.

See one illustration below:

(type_name) expression

You may also wish to learn from a situation where a floating point operation takes place. In such a scenario, you have the cast operator causing a split of an integer variable, actually being done by another. Look at the illustration here below:

#include <stdio.h> #include <stdio.h> main() { int sum = 17, count = 5; double mean; mean = (double) sum / count; printf("Value of mean : %f\n", mean);

The result returned after compilation and also execution of the code laid out above is as follows:

Value of mean : 3.400000

What you need to know at this point is that the program's cast operator takes priority, or has precedence over any integer division or division of any other sort. Consequently, the sum value is straightaway converted into type double; and only after that is it divided following count with a double value.

At times, however, you have type conversions that are implicit, being done automatically by the C compiler. Other times, the type conversions happening explicitly via the employment of the program cast operator. Good practice calls for you to engage the cast operator when you need to make type conversions.

How the integer promotion works
Integer promotion in C is the simple process whereby integer type values *smaller* than *int*, or otherwise *unsigned int*, happen to

undergo conversion so that they become either *int*, or alternatively, *unsigned int*.

Here is an example where you add a character accompanied by an integer:

#include <stdio.h> main() { int i = 17; char c = 'c'; / ascii values is 99 */ int sum; sum = i + c; printf("value of sum : %d/n", sum);
}*

Have you any idea what result you get after compilation and subsequent execution of the code just above? Here it is:

Value of sum : 116

Chapter 13:
Benefits Of Using The C Language

It is an established fact that C, as a programming language, is very popular, in spite of the fact that it came into the market more than three decades ago. It is popular too notwithstanding the emergence of newer programming languages. A beginner may wonder: What is it that attracts users to pick C and not any other programming language, or in some cases, in addition?

Here are some of the positive things users have said about C:

1. The C language provides a foundation for several other programming languages. Not only does it have a lot in common with its newer variations, like C++ and others, but other computer languages have picked fundamental principles from it. For that reason, C is taken to be the main building block for many computer languages existing in the market today.

2. The C programming language is rich in data types and has a wide range of operators. These operators are not just many but they are also very powerful in their execution of commands and functions. It is for this reason that many users have found C to be highly efficient, impressively fast, and also pretty easy to comprehend and use.

3. C is one computer language that you can aptly term portable. What does that portability entail? Well, the C language is one that you can write purposely for one computer, and then you find it easy to run and use on an entirely different computer. Often you are able to do that

without having to alter a thing, and if it is necessary to make some changes, they are often minimal.

4. The C programming language has a range of keywords that you can remember with ease. They are just 32 in number. However, C has the advantage of having built in functions, and these make the use of C all the more efficient. C has at its disposal a reasonable number of standard functions, and these enable users to develop programs with relative ease.

5. C can be said to be versatile. With the great number of functions that it spools from its library, it does not only extend itself as need be, but it also enables the user to add personalized functions to the library with relative ease. On the overall, C makes programming easy whether you are a beginner or a veteran.

6. The C programming language is among the best structured languages in use in the computer world. For that reason, as a user, you are able to think of a challenge in terms of C's function modules; or what you might call blocks.

Being well structured brings other advantages. For starters, being able to fit a problem to where it belongs in terms of function blocks, means you can rectify the problem faster. Also the fact that C is an assembly of modules making a whole program means understanding and dealing with the entire program is easy. By the same token, it becomes easy for someone to debug, test and also maintain this modular structure that is the C programming language.

7. C is procedure oriented

    Where does the advantage lie in this case? Well, it is in your ability to create your customized procedures or even functions, which you can then apply to suit your environment, executing your tasks as you deem appropriate.

    Another benefit that comes with being proccdure oriented is that of ease of learning. This is because C adheres to specific algorithms in executing your statements.
8. The compilation speed experienced in C is far ahead of other programming languages. In actual fact, C's compiler is capable of compiling about a thousand code lines in one or two seconds. The speed is further enhanced by optimization of the code making execution exemplary fast.
9. C's syntax is easy to understand for its language. You will find its keywords mainly in English, which makes it easy for many users to remember them. Some examples of English words in the syntax are switch; if; else; and so on.
10. The C programming languages accords you great preparation for other programming languages. Once you master C, you are in a position to easily learn application development.

The Challenges Faced By Users

In most cases, there is more than one side to an issue. In our case, to this highly popular programming language. Good and handy as it is, the C language does present some challenges sometimes. Here they are:

1. The C programming language does not have Object Oriented Programming System, otherwise referred to as OOPS. Be that as it may, developers of C have gotten over that hitch through development of the more modern C++, a variant of the original C.
2. C does not avail runtime checking
3. The rules of C are not very stringent especially when it comes to type checking. That is why you can easily overlook an integer value.
4. There is a challenge relating to floating data type
5. The C programming language also fails to have the namespace concept
6. It also fails to have the constructor concept as well as the destructor concept.
7. Looking at the whole picture of advantages gauged against the disadvantages, it is clear that the advantages outweigh the challenges. In actual fact, a good number of the challenges are somewhat lightweight and users are able to live with them without jeopardizing their work or use.

Conclusion

How great it is to finally have a book with simple tips on the C programming language! Everyone who has wanted to learn what the C language is all about can now learn that from this book, *C Programming: The Ultimate Guide For Beginners*.

If you have completed reading it, I hope you now understand the reason C is so popular amongst programmers and other computer users who are technology savvy. I also hope that you have learnt specifically the type of data C handles and how it does it; how it stores its files and how you can retrieve them; and all the numerous other details that make the C programming language popular over many other computer languages in the market.

It is our hope that you have found this book a helpful guide.

Resources and Attributions

1. *After All These Years, the World is Still Powered by C Programming*: https://www.toptal.com/c/after-all-these-years-the-world-is-still-powered-by-c-programming
2. *The 10 Most Powerful Supercomputers*: https://www.weforum.org/agenda/2015/07/10-most-powerful-supercomputers/
3. *Where is My Linux GNU C or GCC Compilers Are Installed?* http://www.cyberciti.biz/faq/locate-linux-gnu-c-or-gcc-compiler-location/
4. developer.apple.com/technologies/tools/
5. *Data types in C language*: http://www.studytonight.com/c/datatype-in-c.php
6. *C 32 keywords*: http://www.c4learn.com/c-programming/c-keywords/
7. *C Programming Keywords and Identifiers*: https://www.google.com/#q=double+keywords+in+c+language
8. *Escape sequences in C*: https://en.wikipedia.org/wiki/Escape_sequences_in_C
9. *The C Preprocessor*: https://www.cs.cf.ac.uk/Dave/C/node14.html
10. *Operators in C Language*: http://www.studytonight.com/c/operators-in-c.php
11. *C programming while and do...while loop*: http://www.programiz.com/c-programming/c-do-while-loops
12. *C-Function*: http://fresh2refresh.com/c-programming/c-function/

13. The crazy programmer:
http://www.thecrazyprogrammer.com/2013/07/what-are-advantages-and-disadvantages.html

14. C Language Advantages and Disadvantages : C Language Features: http://latest-technology-guide.blogspot.co.ke/2012/12/c-language-advantages-and-disadvantages.html

Printed in Great Britain
by Amazon